Boaters One Pot Cookbook

The Boaters One Pot Cookbook was produced with recipes supplied to me by boaters. I have included their names and boat names on each recipe.

Many of the recipes do not have exact measurements of ingredients as the boating lifestyle dictates you often put a meal together based on what you have to hand.

I have picked 50 varied recipes and also included 26 pages to enter your own recipes.

I would like to thank all of the boaters, and land-lubbers that contacted me and contributed to this book.

 I hope you enjoy

Happy Cruising!

Greek Chicken with Lemon Rice

RECIPE SUPPLIED BY: MARIE

ABOARD : HONEY BADGER

Ingredients

CHICKEN AND MARINADE
5 CHICKEN THIGHS, SKIN ON, BONE IN (ABOUT 1 KG / 2 LB)
1 - 2 LEMONS, USE THE ZEST + 4 TBSP LEMON JUICE
1 TBSP DRIED OREGANO
4 GARLIC CLOVES, MINCED
1/2 TSP SALT
RICE
1 1/2 TBSP OLIVE OIL, SEPARATED
1 SMALL ONION, FINELY DICED
1 CUP (180G) LONG GRAIN RICE , UNCOOKED
1 1/2 CUPS (375 ML) CHICKEN BROTH / STOCK
3/4 CUP (185 ML) WATER
1 TBSP DRIED OREGANO
3/4 TSP SALT
BLACK PEPPER
GARNISH
FINELY CHOPPED PARSLEY OR OREGANO (OPTIONAL)
FRESH LEMON ZEST (HIGHLY RECOMMENDED)

Method

COMBINE THE CHICKEN AND MARINADE INGREDIENTS IN A ZIPLOCK BAG AND SET ASIDE FOR AT LEAST 20 MINUTES BUT PREFERABLY OVERNIGHT.
TO COOK
PREHEAT OVEN TO 180°C/350°F.
REMOVE CHICKEN FROM MARINADE, BUT RESERVE THE MARINADE.
HEAT 1/2 TBSP OLIVE OIL IN A DEEP, HEAVY BASED PAN OVER MEDIUM HIGH HEAT.
PLACE THE CHICKEN IN THE PAN, SKIN SIDE DOWN, AND COOK UNTIL GOLDEN BROWN, THEN TURN AND COOK THE OTHER SIDE UNTIL GOLDEN BROWN. REMOVE THE CHICKEN AND SET ASIDE.
POUR OFF FAT AND WIPE THE PAN WITH A SCRUNCHED UP BALL OF PAPER TOWEL (TO REMOVE BLACK BITS), THEN RETURN TO THE STOVE.
HEAT 1 TBSP OLIVE OIL IN THE PAN OVER MEDIUM HIGH HEAT. ADD THE ONION AND SAUTÉ FOR A FEW MINUTES UNTIL TRANSLUCENT. THEN ADD THE REMAINING RICE INGREDIENTS AND RESERVED MARINADE.
LET THE LIQUID COME TO A SIMMER AND LET IT SIMMER FOR 30 SECONDS. PLACE THE CHICKEN ON TOP THEN PLACE A LID (OR ALUMINUM FOIL)ON THE PAN BAKE IN THE OVEN FOR 35 MINUTES. THEN REMOVE THE LID AND BAKE FOR A FURTHER 10 MINUTES, OR UNTIL ALL THE LIQUID IS ABSORBED AND THE RICE IS TENDER (SO 45 MINUTES IN TOTAL).
REMOVE FROM THE OVEN AND ALLOW TO REST FOR 5 TO 10 MINUTES BEFORE SERVING, GARNISHED WITH PARSLEY OR OREGANO AND FRESH LEMON ZEST, IF DESIRED.

Sweet Potato & Butternut Squash Curry

RECIPE SUPPLIED BY: BRENDAN
ABOARD : LADY JANE

Ingredients

1 BUTTERNUT SQUASH
2 SWEET POTATOES
1 RED PEPPER
2 ONIONS
3 CRUSHED GARLIC CLOVES
1 INCH ROOT GINGER, PEELED AND CHOPPED
1 TIN BUTTER BEANS
400 G BROCCOLI FLORETS
400 G TINNED TOMATOES
1 TSP GARAM MASALA
1/2 TSP GROUND CUMIN
1/2 TSP GROUND CHILLI POWDER
3 CARDAMOM PODS
1 CLOVE, BLENDED TO A FINE POWDER
250 ML NATURAL YOGHURT
RAPESEED OIL SPRAY

Method

PRE-HEAT THE OVEN TO 200°C. CUT THE SWEET POTATO, AND BUTTERNUT SQUASH INTO BITE SIZED CHUNKS. LAY ON ROASTING TRAY, AND SPRAY LIGHTLY WITH RAPESEED OIL. ROAST IN THE OVEN FOR 30 MINUTES UNTIL SOFTENED.

SLICE THE ONIONS AND SOFTEN IN A LARGE PAN WITH A FINE SPRAY OF RAPESEED OIL. ONCE SOFTENED, ADD SPICES, FRESH GINGER, AND GARLIC INTO THE PAN. ADD THE ROASTED SWEET POTATO, AND BUTTERNUT SQUASH, ALONG WITH THE CHOPPED PEPPERS AND BUTTER BEANS.

ADD THE TINNED TOMATOES, THEN REFILL THE CAN WITH WATER AND ADD TO THE PAN. ALLOW TO REDUCE SLIGHTLY, ADD BROCCOLI FLORETS AND SIMMER FOR 15-20 MINUTES UNTIL ALL VEGETABLES ARE SOFTENED.

AT THE END OF COOKING SLOWLY STIR IN THE NATURAL YOGHURT. SERVE WITH NAAN OR PITTA BREAD.

Cheesy Beef Macaroni

RECIPE SUPPLIED BY: MARIE
ABOARD : HONEY BADGER

Ingredients

500 G OF BEEF MINCE
10 MLS (2 TEASPOONS) OF PAPRIKA
TWO CLOVES OF GARLIC, MINCED
ONE ONION, MINCED
SALT AND PEPPER TO TASTE
750 MLS (3 CUPS) BEEF STOCK
250 MLS (1 CUP) OF MILK
15 MLS (1 TABLESPOON) MARMITE
15 MLS (1 TABLESPOON) DIJON OR OTHER MUSTARD
2 CUPS DRY MACARONI
200 GRAMS (2 CUPS) GRATED CHEDDAR CHEESE

Method

BROWN THE MINCE BEEF IN A HEAVY POT THAT HAS A LID.
WHEN THE BEEF IS MOSTLY BROWNED,
ADD THE ONION AND THE GARLIC
CONTINUE TO FRY UNTIL THE ONION HAS SOFTENED.
STIR IN THE PAPRIKA, SALT, PEPPER, STOCK, MILK, MARMITE, AND MUSTARD.
BRING TO A SIMMER, THEN STIR IN THE PASTA. COVER WITH A LID, REDUCE HEAT AND SIMMER FOR FIVE MINUTES.
AT THE FIVE MINUTE MARK LIFT THE LID,
GIVE THE MIXTURE A STIR AND SEE IF YOU NEED ANY EXTRA LIQUID AND TEST THE PASTA FOR DONE-NESS
WHEN THE PASTA IS COOKED TO YOUR LIKING, TURN OFF THE HEAT, STIR THE CHEESE AND THEN RECOVER THE POT.
LET STAND COVERED FOR 10 TO 15 MINUTES TO LET THE SAUCE THICKEN AND THE FLAVOURS MELD.

Vegetarian Sausage Casserole

RECIPE SUPPLIED BY: PHILLIP
ABOARD : SWEET WILLIAM

Ingredients

8 VEGETARIAN SAUSAGES
OLIVE OIL
1 RED ONION
1 LARGE RED PEPPER
2 GARLIC CLOVES CRUSHED
1 1/2 TSP SMOKED PAPRIKA
2 TBSP SUN-DRIED TOMATO PASTE
800 G CHOPPED CANNED TOMATOES
800 G CANNED CANNELLINI BEANS
2 TSP DRIED THYME
2 TSP DRIED OREGANO
2 TSP SUGAR OPTIONAL

Method

HEAT SOME OLIVE OIL IN A LARGE CASSEROLE. GENTLY FRY THE SAUSAGES UNTIL SLIGHTLY BROWN.
ADD FINELY SLICED RED ONION, SLICED RED PEPPER, CRUSHED GARLIC, SMOKED PAPRIKA AND SUN-DRIED TOMATO PASTE. FRY ALL TOGETHER FOR ANOTHER 3 MINUTES.
ADD CHOPPED TOMATOES, DRAINED CANNELLINI BEANS, THYME AND OREGANO TO THE CASSEROLE.
COOK FOR 10 MINS COVERED, THEN 10 MINS UNCOVERED UNTIL RED PEPPER IS SOFT.
SEASON TO TASTE, ADD SUGAR IF REQUIRED
SERVE WITH MASHED POTATOES WITH CHOPPED PARSLEY ON TOP.

One Pot Sunday Lunch

RECIPE SUPPLIED BY: CARMEL
ABOARD : BIG EASY

Ingredients

3 TBSP. OLIVE OIL
2 TBSP. CIDER VINEGAR
3 TBSP. GOLDEN SYRUP SUGAR
1 TBSP. ROUGHLY CHOPPED THYME LEAVES
4 PORK SAUSAGES, TWISTED IN HALF & CUT
8 THIN RASHERS BACON
4 CHICKEN THIGHS
6 MEDIUM NEW POTATOES, HALVED LENGTHWAYS
8 SMALL CARROTS, PEELED
2 PARSNIPS, PEELED & HALVED LENGTHWAYS
2 MEDIUM RED ONIONS, PEELED, QUARTERED
SALT & FRESHLY GROUND BLACK PEPPER

Method

PREHEAT THE OVEN TO 200°C/GAS MARK 6.
MIX TOGETHER THE OLIVE OIL, VINEGAR, SUGAR, THYME AND A
GENEROUS AMOUNT OF SALT AND PEPPER.
NEXT, WRAP EACH SAUSAGE HALF IN BACON, THEN PLACE IN A LARGE
ROASTING TIN OR TWO SMALLER ONES SO AS NOT TO OVERCROWD
EVERYTHING. ADD THE CHICKEN, POTATOES, CARROTS, PARSNIPS AND
ONIONS, THEN DRIZZLE OVER THE OLIVE OIL MIXTURE AND RUB
EVERYTHING WELL TO COAT, ENSURING THE CHICKEN IS SKIN-SIDE
UPPERMOST.
ROAST ON THE MIDDLE SHELF OF THE OVEN FOR 35 TO 40 MINUTES,
TURNING THE VEGETABLES AND SAUSAGES HALFWAY THROUGH AND
BASTING EVERYTHING WITH THE JUICES. WHEN THE CHICKEN SKIN IS
CRISP AND GOLDEN AND THE VEGETABLES ARE GLAZED AND TENDER,
THE DISH IS READY. REMOVE AND SERVE.

Corned Beef Hash

RECIPE SUPPLIED BY: PETER
ABOARD : OLIVIA

Ingredients

2 TBSP VEGETABLE OIL
1 ONION, FINELY CHOPPED
567G CAN NEW POTATOES, DRAINED
130G CAN CORNED BEEF
2 FREE-RANGE EGGS
SPLASH WORCESTERSHIRE SAUCE
FRESHLY GROUND BLACK PEPPER

Method

HEAT THE OIL IN A MEDIUM FRYING PAN AND GENTLY FRY THE ONION FOR 3-4 MINUTES, OR UNTIL LIGHTLY BROWNED.
ADD THE POTATOES AND USE A POTATO MASHER TO ROUGHLY CRUSH THEM. FRY OVER A MEDIUM HEAT FOR 5 MINUTES, OR UNTIL THE ONION IS SOFTENED AND THE POTATOES ARE HOT AND BROWNED IN PLACES, STIRRING REGULARLY.
ADD THE CORNED BEEF AND BREAK UP ROUGHLY WITH A SPOON. COOK FOR 3-4 MINUTES, OR UNTIL HOT, STIRRING OCCASIONALLY.
MAKE TWO HOLES IN THE CORNED BEEF AND POTATO MIXTURE AND BREAK AN EGG INTO EACH ONE. FRY FOR 2-3 MINUTES, OR UNTIL THE WHITES ARE SET BUT THE YOLKS REMAIN RUNNY.
SERVE THE CORNED BEEF HASH ON WARMED PLATES, TOPPED WITH THE FRIED EGGS. SHAKE WORCESTERSHIRE SAUCE OVER AND SEASON WITH PEPPER.

One Pot Fish Stew

RECIPE SUPPLIED BY: NIKKI
ABOARD : NORTHERN STAR

Ingredients

1 TBSP OLIVE OIL
1 BULB FENNEL, THINLY SLICED
3 CLOVES GARLIC, THINLY SLICED
1 TBSP FENNEL SEEDS
1 TBSP SWEET SMOKED PAPRIKA
1 TBSP TOMATO PURÉE
150ML WHITE WINE
400G TIN CHERRY TOMATOES
400G TIN BUTTER BEANS, RINSED AND DRAINED
100G KALE, CHOPPED, TOUGH STALKS DISCARDED
180G RAW PRAWNS
300G SKINLESS WHITE FISH (SUCH AS COD, COLEY OR HADDOCK), CUT INTO 4CM PIECES
50G FETA, CRUMBLED
A SMALL BUNCH FLAT-LEAF PARSLEY, CHOPPED

Method

HEAT THE OLIVE OIL IN A LARGE, LIDDED, NON-STICK FRYING PAN OVER A MEDIUM-HIGH HEAT AND COOK THE FENNEL FOR 4-5 MINUTES OR UNTIL CARAMELISED. TURN DOWN THE HEAT AND ADD THE GARLIC, FENNEL SEEDS, PAPRIKA AND TOMATO PURÉE, AND COOK FOR 1 MINUTE. POUR IN THE WINE AND BUBBLE FOR A MINUTE BEFORE ADDING THE TOMATOES, BEANS AND HALF A TIN OF WATER. SEASON LIGHTLY AND SIMMER FOR 15 MINUTES.

SEASON THE SAUCE AGAIN, IF NEEDED, AND STIR THROUGH THE KALE. NESTLE IN THE PRAWNS AND FISH PIECES, PUT ON THE LID AND SIMMER GENTLY FOR 5 MINUTES UNTIL THE FISH IS JUST COOKED THROUGH. SPRINKLE OVER THE FETA AND PARSLEY, AND SERVE WITH CRUSTY BREAD.

Pan Haggerty

RECIPE SUPPLIED BY: BRIAN
ABOARD : ALLSTAR

Ingredients

1 TBSP VEGETABLE OIL
250G STREAKY BACON
6 POTATOES, THINLY SLICED INTO ROUNDS
2 ONIONS, THINLY SLICED
5 CARROTS, PEELED AND THINLY SLICED
500ML CHICKEN STOCK
150G CHEDDAR, GRATED
SALT AND FRESHLY GROUND BLACK PEPPER
CRUSTY BREAD, TO SERVE

Method

HEAT THE VEGETABLE OIL IN A DEEP PAN. FRY THE BACON FOR UNTIL
GOLDEN-BROWN AND SLIGHTLY CRISP. REMOVE FROM THE PAN AND
SET ASIDE TO DRAIN.
IN THE SAME PAN, ARRANGE A LAYER OF THE SLICED POTATOES IN THE
BOTTOM. COVER THE POTATOES WITH A LAYER OF SLICED ONIONS,
THEN A LAYER OF SLICED CARROTS. LAYER OVER SOME OF THE BACON.
SEASON WITH SALT AND PEPPER.
REPEAT THE PROCESS WITH THE REMAINING POTATOES, ONIONS,
CARROTS AND BACON, FINISHING WITH A LAYER OF POTATOES ON TOP.
SEASON WITH SALT AND PEPPER.
POUR IN THE CHICKEN STOCK SO THAT ALL OF THE INGREDIENTS ARE
COVERED, THEN BRING TO THE BOIL. COVER THE PAN WITH A LID AND
REDUCE THE HEAT TO A SIMMER. SIMMER FOR 15-25 MINUTES, OR
UNTIL THE POTATOES AND CARROTS ARE TENDER.
PREHEAT THE GRILL TO HIGH. UNCOVER THE PAN AND SPRINKLE OVER
THE GRATED CHEESE. GRILL FOR 5-6 MINUTES, OR UNTIL THE CHEESE
IS BUBBLING AND GOLDEN-BROWN.
TO SERVE, SPOON INTO BOWLS AND SERVE WITH SOME CRUSTY BREAD
TO MOP UP THE JUICES.

One Pot Chorizo Pasta

RECIPE SUPPLIED BY: BILLY
ABOARD : FLOATY BOATY

Ingredients

150G CHORIZO, ROUGHLY CHOPPED
4 GARLIC CLOVES, FINELY CHOPPED
4 PEPPERS (MIXTURE OF RED AND YELLOW), HALVED,
DESEEDED AND ROUGHLY CHOPPED
160G BUTTON MUSHROOMS, HALVED
400G TIN CHOPPED TOMATOES
3 TBSP TOMATO PURÉE
1 TSP DRIED RED CHILLI FLAKES
2 TBSP RED WINE VINEGAR
450G SPAGHETTI, BROKEN IN HALF
1 LITRE BOILING WATER
SEA SALT AND FRESHLY GROUND BLACK PEPPER
1 LARGE HANDFUL BASIL LEAVES, ROUGHLY CHOPPED
30G PARMESAN, FRESHLY GRATED

Method

HEAT A LARGE, DEEP-SIDED CASSEROLE OR FRYING PAN OVER A HIGH
HEAT, ADD THE CHORIZO AND COOK FOR 2–3 MINUTES.
ADD THE GARLIC, PEPPERS AND BUTTON MUSHROOMS AND COOK FOR
ANOTHER 2–3 MINUTES, STIRRING OCCASIONALLY.
ADD THE CHOPPED TOMATOES, TOMATO PURÉE, CHILLI FLAKES AND
RED WINE VINEGAR. STIR IN THE SPAGHETTI, POUR IN THE BOILING
WATER AND STIR WELL.
BRING TO THE BOIL, REDUCE THE HEAT, COVER WITH A LID AND
SIMMER FOR 12–15 MINUTES, OR UNTIL THE PASTA IS AL DENTE, AND
THE LIQUID HAS REDUCED TO A THICK SAUCE. STIR THE MIXTURE
OCCASIONALLY TO MAKE SURE THAT THE PASTA IS UNDER THE LIQUID
AND NOT STICKING TOGETHER.
STIR IN THREE QUARTERS OF THE BASIL ADD BLACK PEPPER
SERVE WITH THE PARMESAN AND REMAINING BASIL.

Vegetarian Mushroom Stroganoff

RECIPE SUPPLIED BY: DOT
ABOARD : LAND DWELLER

Ingredients

1 SMALL ONION, SLICED AND QUARTERED
10 OUNCES (280 G) LARGE MUSHROOMS, CUT IN HALF OR FOURTHS
8 OUNCES (225 G) DRY PASTA;
4 CUPS IMITATION "BEEF-FLAVORED" BROTH (OR USE VEGETABLE BROTH)
2 TABLESPOONS NUTRITIONAL YEAST
1/4 TEASPOON FRESHLY GROUND BLACK PEPPER, PLUS MORE TO TASTE IF NEEDED
85GM CASHEW BUTTER OR OTHER VEGGIE BUTTER
1 TABLESPOON LEMON JUICE
1/4 – 1/2 TEASPOON SALT (OPTIONAL)
2 TABLESPOONS PARSLEY, CHOPPED

Method

SAUTÉ THE ONION: ADD 60 ML OF WATER TO A LARGE POT OVER MEDIUM HEAT. ADD IN THE SLICED ONIONS AND COOK UNTIL TRANSLUCENT, ABOUT 3 TO 5 MINUTES. YOU CAN ALSO SAUTÉ THE ONIONS IN 1 TABLESPOON OF OIL INSTEAD OF WATER, IF YOU WISH.

COOK THE PASTA: ADD IN THE PASTA, MUSHROOMS, BEEF-FLAVORED BROTH, NUTRITIONAL YEAST, AND BLACK PEPPER. BRING TO A BOIL OVER HIGH HEAT, THEN REDUCE THE HEAT TO MEDIUM-LOW AND LET SIMMER FOR 10-15 MINUTES, STIRRING OCCASIONALLY TO ENSURE NOTHING STICKS TO THE BOTTOM OF THE PAN.

MAKE IT CREAMY: TURN THE HEAT OFF, THEN STIR IN THE CASHEW BUTTER AND LEMON JUICE UNTIL EVERYTHING IS WELL INCORPORATED. TASTE THE PASTA AND ADD ANY ADDITIONAL SALT, IF NECESSARY.

SERVE: TOP WITH FRESHLY CHOPPED PARSLEY AND BLACK PEPPER, AND SERVE WARM. STORE ANY LEFTOVERS IN AN AIRTIGHT CONTAINER IN THE FRIDGE FOR UP TO ONE WEEK.

Chicken & Peanut Butter

RECIPE SUPPLIED BY: MADDY
ABOARD : SWEET PEA

Ingredients

1 TBSP OLIVE OR VEGETABLE OIL
4 LARGE CHICKEN THIGHS, SKIN REMOVED AND BONELESS,
EACH CUT INTO 8 CHUNKS
2 LARGE SHALLOTS, PEELED AND SLICED
2 RED PEPPERS, CUT INTO LONG SLICES
1 RED CHILLI, SEEDS REMOVED & CHOPPED
3 GARLIC CLOVES, FINELY SLICED
400ML TIN COCONUT MILK
4 TBSP PEANUT BUTTER (SMOOTH OR CRUNCHY)
2 LIMES, JUICE ONLY
2 TBSP SOY SAUCE
2 TBSP CHOPPED FRESH CORIANDER LEAVES, TO GARNISH

Method

HEAT THE OIL IN A LARGE FRYING PAN OVER A HIGH HEAT.
FRY THE CHICKEN FOR 5 MINUTES, STIRRING EVERY 30 SECONDS.
TURN THE HEAT DOWN TO LOW, ADD THE SHALLOTS, RED PEPPERS,
CHILLI AND GARLIC AND COOK FOR 5 MINUTES, OR UNTIL SOFTENED.
STIR IN THE COCONUT MILK AND PEANUT BUTTER.
HALF-FILL THE COCONUT MILK TIN WITH WATER AND ADD TO THE PAN.
BRING TO THE BOIL, THEN COVER WITH A LID AND COOK OVER A
MEDIUM HEAT FOR 7 MINUTES, STIRRING OCCASIONALLY, UNTIL THE
CHICKEN IS COOKED.
IF YOU WANT TO THICKEN THE PEANUT BUTTER SAUCE, REMOVE THE
LID AND BOIL TO REDUCE THE SAUCE TO A COATING CONSISTENCY.
STIR IN THE LIME JUICE AND SOY SAUCE. TASTE AND ADJUST THE
SEASONING IF NECESSARY – ADD MORE SOY SAUCE OR MORE LIME
JUICE TO BALANCE OUT THE SWEET-SALTINESS.
GARNISH WITH THE CHOPPED CORIANDER, IF USING, AND SERVE WITH
WHITE RICE AND/OR STEAMED GREENS.

13

Pork Chop Supper

RECIPE SUPPLIED BY: ANDY

ABOARD : ARTIMIS

Ingredients

TABLESPOON BUTTER
4 PORK LOIN CHOPS
3 MEDIUM POTATOES, CUT INTO SMALL WEDGES
3 MEDIUM CARROTS, CUT INTO 1/2-INCH SLICES
1 MEDIUM ONION, CUT INTO WEDGES
1 CAN CONDENSED CREAM OF MUSHROOM SOUP
1/2 CUP WATER
OPTIONAL: CRACKED BLACK PEPPER AND CHOPPED FRESH
PARSLEY

Method

IN A LARGE CAST-IRON OR OTHER HEAVY PAN, HEAT BUTTER OVER
MEDIUM HEAT. BROWN PORK CHOPS ON BOTH SIDES; REMOVE FROM
PAN, RESERVING JUICES.

IN SAME PAN, SAUTE VEGETABLES IN JUICES UNTIL LIGHTLY BROWNED.
WHISK TOGETHER SOUP AND WATER.

STIR INTO VEGETABLES. BRING TO A BOIL. REDUCE HEAT; SIMMER,
COVERED, JUST UNTIL VEGETABLES ARE TENDER, 15-20 MINUTES.

ADD CHOPS; COOK, COVERED FOR 8-10 MINUTES. REMOVE FROM HEAT;
LET STAND 5 MINUTES.

IF DESIRED, SPRINKLE WITH PEPPER AND PARSLEY.

Leek Curry

RECIPE SUPPLIED BY: STEPH
ABOARD : JOHNNY B

Ingredients

600 G LEEKS
350 G TOMATOES
VEGETABLE OIL
4 DRY CURRY LEAVES
3 GARLIC CLOVES (GRATED)
1 TSP FRESHLY GRATED GINGER
¾ TSP TURMERIC
1 TBSP MILD CURRY POWDER
400 ML COCONUT MILK
400 G CHICKPEAS
3/4 TSP GARAM MASALA
LEMON JUICE , SALT (TO TASTE)
SERVE WITH: BASMATI RIC, NAAN BREAD & CHILLIS

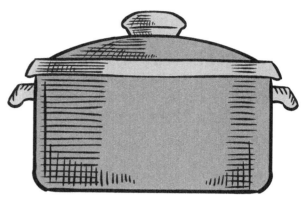

Method

CUT THE LEEKS INTO 1 CM CHUNKS AND DICE TOMATOES
HEAT SOME VEGETABLE OIL IN A LARGE SAUCEPAN. ADD THE CURRY
LEAVES AND FRY THEM UNTIL THEY CRACKLE
ADD THE LEEKS AND TOMATOES AND COOK FOR 5 MINS UNTIL SOFT.
ADD GRATED GARLIC CLOVES, FRESHLY GRATED GINGER, TURMERIC &
MILD CURRY POWDER. STIR TOGETHER & COOK FOR FURTHER 5 MINS.
ADD THE COCONUT MILK AND DRAINED CHICKPEAS. COOK HALF
COVERED UNDER MEDIUM HEAT FOR ANOTHER 10-15MINS UNTIL THE
LEEKS ARE COOKED.
ADD THE GARAM MASALA & COOK FOR ANOTHER COUPLE OF MINUTES.
SEASON TO TASTE WITH LEMON JUICE AND SALT.
SERVE THIS LEEK CURRY WITH BASMATI RICE TOPPED WITH FRESHLY
CHOPPED CORIANDER AND CHILLIES & NAAN BREAD.

Chorizo & Bean Stew

RECIPE SUPPLIED BY: JOYCE
ABOARD : MISTY MORNING

Ingredients

200G CHORIZO, CHOPPED
SPLASH OF OLIVE OIL
ONION, PEELED AND DICED
1 CLOVE OF CHOPPED GARLIC
1 TIN (400G) CHOPPED TOMATOES
2 TINS (800G) CANNELLINI BEANS
SALT & PEPPER
FRESH PARSLEY
1 TEASPOON PAPRIKA

Method

HEAT A SPLASH OF OLIVE OIL IN A LARGE PAN OVER A MEDIUM HEAT AND ADD THE CHORIZO FOR A COUPLE OF MINUTES UNTIL THEY BEGIN TO RELEASE THEIR NATURAL OILS.
ADD IN THE ONIONS AND FRY FOR A FURTHER COUPLE OF MINUTES UNTIL THEY BEGIN TO COLOUR.
ADD THE GARLIC AND SEASON WITH A TEASPOON OF PAPRIKA OR A PINCH OF CAYENNE PEPPER FOR EXTRA SPICE. COOK FOR A FURTHER MINUTE.
DRAIN AND RINSE THE BEANS. YOU CAN USE CANNELLINI BEANS, BUTTER BEANS, CHICKPEAS OR A MIXTURE
ADD THE BEANS TO THE PAN WITH THE TIN OF CHOPPED TOMATOES.
SEASON TO TASTE WITH SALT, PEPPER AND CHOPPED FRESH PARSLEY OR ROSEMARY. YOU COULD ALSO ADD FLAVOUR WITH SOME DRIED OREGANO AND/OR A SPLASH OF WORCESTERSHIRE SAUCE.
STIR WELL AND SIMMER FOR AROUND 15 MINUTES UNTIL THE STEW HAS THICKENED TO DESIRED CONSISTENCY.
STIR OCCASIONALLY AND ADD A LITTLE WATER IF THE STEW GETS TOO THICK.
SERVE WITH CRUSTY BREAD OR JACKET POTATOES

Broccoli And Cheddar Frittata

RECIPE SUPPLIED BY: MARY
ABOARD : ROYAL DUTCH

Ingredients

9 EGGS
1 CAN CONDENSED BROCCOLI SOUP
1 TABLESPOON BUTTER
1 CUP OF MUSHROOMS, COARSELY CHOPPED
1 LARGE ONION, CHOPPED
1 COURGETTE, COARSELY CHOPPED
1/2 CUP GRATED CHEDDAR CHEESE
3 SPRING ONIONS, CHOPPED

Method

BEAT THE EGGS AND SOUP IN A MEDIUM BOWL WITH A FORK OR WHISK. SEASON WITH SALT AND PEPPER.
HEAT THE BUTTER IN A 12-INCH OVENPROOF NONSTICK PAN OVER MEDIUM HEAT. ADD THE MUSHROOMS, ONION AND COURGETTE AND COOK UNTIL TENDER. STIR IN THE EGG MIXTURE. REDUCE THE HEAT TO LOW. COOK FOR 5 MINUTES OR UNTIL THE EGG MIXTURE IS ALMOST SET BUT STILL MOIST.
SPRINKLE THE CHEESE OVER THE EGG MIXTURE. COOK THE FRITTATA WITH THE TOP 4 INCHES FROM THE HEAT FOR 2 MINUTES OR UNTIL THE TOP IS GOLDEN BROWN. SPRINKLE WITH THE SPRING ONIONS BEFORE SERVING.

One Pot Lasagne

RECIPE SUPPLIED BY: ELLEN
ABOARD : MARY ANNE

Ingredients

1 TABLESPOON OLIVE OIL
3 ITALIAN SAUSAGE, CASING REMOVED
1 CAN CHOPPED TOMATOES
1 CAN TOMATO SAUCE
1 TEASPOON DRIED OREGANO
1 TEASPOON DRIED BASIL
1/2 TEASPOON GARLIC POWDER
1/2 TEASPOON CRUSHED RED PEPPER FLAKES,
8 OUNCES PASTA
SALT AND GROUND BLACK PEPPER, TO TASTE
1 CUP SHREDDED MOZZARELLA CHEESE
1/4 CUP FRESHLY GRATED PARMESAN
1 CUP RICOTTA CHEESE
2 TABLESPOONS CHOPPED FRESH PARSLEY LEAVES

Method

HEAT OLIVE OIL IN A LARGE PAN OVER MEDIUM HIGH HEAT.
ADD ITALIAN SAUSAGE & COOK UNTIL BROWNED,
BREAK UP THE SAUSAGE AS IT COOKS; DRAIN EXCESS FAT.
STIR IN DICED TOMATOES, TOMATO SAUCE, OREGANO, BASIL, GARLIC
POWDER AND RED PEPPER FLAKES.
SEASON WITH SALT AND PEPPER, TO TASTE.

BRING TO A SIMMER AND STIR IN PASTA AND 2 CUPS WATER. BRING TO
A BOIL; COVER, REDUCE HEAT AND SIMMER UNTIL PASTA IS COOKED
THROUGH, ABOUT 13-15 MINUTES.
REMOVE FROM HEAT. STIR IN MOZZARELLA AND PARMESAN UNTIL WELL
COMBINED,
TOP WITH DOLLOPS OF RICOTTA AND COVER UNTIL HEATED THROUGH,
SERVE IMMEDIATELY, GARNISHED WITH PARSLEY, IF DESIRED.

Onion & Spring Vegetable Pilaf

RECIPE SUPPLIED BY: CHLOE
ABOARD : HEAVEN SENT

Ingredients

2 LARGE ONIONS
50G BUTTER
100G FINE GREEN BEANS, HALVED
2 CLOVES GARLIC, CRUSHED
1 TSP CUMIN SEEDS
1 TSP GROUND CORIANDER
6 PODS CARDAMOM, SQUASHED
1 TSP GROUND TURMERIC
1 BAY LEAF
250G BASMATI RICE
450ML VEGETABLE STOCK
100G FROZEN PEAS, DEFROSTED
100G SPINACH, CHOPPED

Method

PEEL THE ONIONS AND DISCARD THE FIRST TOUGHER OUTER LAYER.
HALVE AND SLICE AS THINLY AS POSSIBLE.
HEAT THE BUTTER IN A LARGE, DEEP, LIDDED FRYING PAN. ADD THE
ONION WITH A GOOD PINCH OF SALT AND COOK OVER A MEDIUM HEAT,
STIRRING, UNTIL REALLY GOLDEN AND CARAMELISED. THIS CAN TAKE
UP TO 30 MINUTES, IT SHOULD BE SOFT ENOUGH TO SQUASH A PIECE
OF ONION BETWEEN YOUR FINGERS.

STIR IN THE GREEN BEANS AND GARLIC, AND COOK FOR 2 MINUTES
THEN STIR IN THE SPICES AND BAY LEAF, IF USING, AND COOK FOR 1
MINUTE.
ADD THE RICE AND STIR UNTIL COATED IN ALL THE SPICES. STIR IN
THE STOCK, PUT ON A LID AND COOK ON A LOW HEAT FOR 15 MINUTES,
STIRRING IN THE PEAS AND SPINACH FOR THE FINAL 3 MINUTES.

One Pot Spaghetti Bolognaise

RECIPE SUPPLIED BY: SARAH
ABOARD : BETTY BOOP

Ingredients

1 STALK CHOPPED CELERY
4 BACON RASHERS, TRIMMED, CHOPPED
2 GARLIC CLOVES, FINELY CHOPPED
600G BEEF MINCE
3 TABLESPOONS TOMATO PUREE
2 X CANS CHOPPED TOMATOES
1 PINT CHICKEN STOCK
6 SPRIGS FRESH THYME
250G SPAGHETTI
1/4 CUP CHOPPED FRESH PARSLEY LEAVES
EXTRA CHOPPED FRESH FLAT-LEAF PARSLEY, TO SERVE
GRATED PARMESAN, TO SERVE

Method

ADD OIL TO A LARGE CASSEROLE DISH OVER MEDIUM HEAT ADD ONION, CARROT AND CELERY. COOK, STIRRING OCCASIONALLY, UNTIL ONION STARTS TO SOFTEN. ADD BACON. COOK UNTIL GOLDEN. ADD GARLIC. STIR TO COMBINE.

ADD MINCE TO DISH. COOK, BREAKING UP MINCE WITH A WOODEN SPOON, UNTIL BROWNED ALL OVER. STIR IN TOMATO PUREE, TOMATOES, STOCK AND THYME SPRIGS. COVER. BRING TO THE BOIL. ADD SPAGHETTI. REDUCE HEAT TO MEDIUM. SIMMER, UNCOVERED, UNTIL SPAGHETTI IS TENDER AND SAUCE HAS THICKENED, STIRRING MIXTURE EVERY 5 MINUTES.
REMOVE POT FROM HEAT. REMOVE AND DISCARD THYME SPRIGS. ADD PARSLEY. SEASON WITH SALT AND PEPPER. STIR TO COMBINE. SERVE TOPPED WITH EXTRA CHOPPED PARSLEY AND PARMESAN.

One Pot Mexican Fish

RECIPE SUPPLIED BY: BRENDAN
ABOARD : MAGGIE

Ingredients

1 TBSP. OLIVE OIL
1 BELL PEPPER, ANY COLOR, THINLY SLICED
1 SMALL ONION, HALVED AND THINLY SLICED
2 GARLIC CLOVES, MINCED
1 CUP SALSA, MILD, MEDIUM, OR HOT
1 X CAN TOMATOES, UNDRAINED
1 TEASPOON CHILI POWDER
1 TEASPOON GROUND CUMIN
1/4 TEASPOON GROUND CORIANDER
1/4 TEASPOON SALT
1 X CAN BLACK BEANS, DRAINED AND RINSED
1 CUP SWEETCORN, FROZEN OR CANNED
1 POUND WHITE FISH,COD,POLLOCK, COLEY
1/2 LIME

Method

IN A LARGE PAN HEAT OLIVE OIL OVER MEDIUM HIGH HEAT.
ADD PEPPERS, ONIONS AND FRY UNTIL SOFT, ABOUT 5 MINUTES.
ADD GARLIC AND FRY 30 SECONDS MORE.
REDUCE HEAT TO MEDIUM LOW, ADD SALSA, TOMATOES, CHILI POWDER,
CUMIN, CORIANDER, AND SALT. SIMMER, UNCOVERED, FOR 5 MINUTES,
ADD BEANS AND CORN, STIR, AND BRING BACK TO A SIMMER.
ADD FISH, COVER AND SIMMER FOR ABOUT 10-15 MINUTES. COOKING
TIME WILL DEPEND ON THICKNESS OF FISH.
LOOK FOR COLOUR INSIDE CHANGING FROM TRANSLUCENT TO OPAQUE.
IF THE SAUCE NEEDS TO THICKEN SLIGHTLY, REMOVE FISH, COVER
LOOSELY WITH FOIL, AND SIMMER SAUCE UNCOVERED 5 MINUTES OR
UNTIL IT'S REDUCED AND THICKENED.
SQUEEZE LIME JUICE OVER FISH. SERVE OVER RICE. TOP FISH WITH
TORTILLA CHIPS, CHEESE, CORIANDER, SOUR CREAM, AND ADDITIONAL
LIME WEDGES.

Butternut Squash And Chickpea Curry

RECIPE SUPPLIED BY: CAROLINE
ABOARD : HAGGERTY

Ingredients

650 G BUTTERNUT SQUASH
3 TOMATOES
2 TBSP VEGETABLE OIL
1 ONION
1 TSP TURMERIC
1 TSP GROUND CUMIN
1 TSP GROUND CORIANDER
2 TSP GARAM MASALA
1/2 TSP GROUND CINNAMON
1 TSP CHILLI POWDER
1 TBSP FRESHLY GRATED GINGER
400 ML COCONUT MILK
250 ML VEGETABLE STOCK
2 GARLIC CLOVES
2 HANDFULS OF BABY SPINACH LEAVES
400 G CAN CHICKPEAS
LIME JUICE TO TASTE
SALT
CHILLI FLAKES TO SERVE – OPTIONAL
FRESH CORIANDER TO SERVE – OPTIONAL

Method

PEEL BUTTERNUT SQUASH & CUT IN 1.5CM DICE.
CUT TOMATOES IN QUARTERS.
HEAT SOME OIL IN A LARGE SAUCEPAN. ADD FINELY CHOPPED ONION, TURMERIC, GROUND CUMIN, GROUND CORIANDER, GARAM MASALA, CINNAMON, CHILLI POWDER AND GRATED GINGER. FRY UNDER MEDIUM HEAT FOR A FEW MINUTES UNTIL ONION IS SOFT.
ADD DICED BUTTERNUT AND QUARTERED TOMATOES. ADD COCONUT MILK, VEGETABLE STOCK AND CRUSHED GARLIC. BRING TO THE BOIL THEN LEAVE TO SIMMER UNCOVERED UNDER MEDIUM HEAT FOR AROUND 20 MINUTES. BUTTERNUT SHOULD BE COOKED BUT STILL HAVE A BITE.
ADD SPINACH AND COOK UNTIL WILTED. THEN ADD DRAINED CHICKPEAS. MIX WELL. SEASON TO TASTE WITH LIME JUICE, SALT & EXTRA CHILLI POWDER IF NEEDED.
SERVE WITH CHILLI FLAKES & CHOPPED FRESH CORIANDER LEAVES.

One Pot French Onion Soup

RECIPE SUPPLIED BY: BERNIE
ABOARD : YORKSHIRE LASS

Ingredients

12 (3/4-INCH-THICK) FRENCH BAGUETTE SLICES
1/4 CUP BUTTER
1.3 KILOS ONIONS, SLICED
3 CLOVES GARLIC, MINCED
1/3 CUP DRY WHITE WINE
6 CUPS BEEF STOCK
4 SPRIGS FRESH THYME
2 BAY LEAVES
2 TEASPOONS BALSAMIC VINEGAR
SALT AND FRESHLY GROUND BLACK PEPPER, TO TASTE
1 1/2 CUPS SHREDDED GRUYÈRE CHEESE
1/2 CUP FRESHLY GRATED PARMESAN

Method

PREHEAT OVEN
PLACE BAGUETTE SLICES ONTO A BAKING SHEET. PLACE INTO OVEN & COOK UNTIL GOLDEN BROWN ON BOTH SIDES, ABOUT 1-2 MINUTES PER SIDE; SET ASIDE.
MELT BUTTER IN A LARGE OVEN-PROOF DISH OVER MEDIUM HEAT. ADD ONIONS, AND COOK, STIRRING OFTEN, UNTIL DEEP GOLDEN BROWN AND CARAMELIZED, ABOUT 30-40 MINUTES.* STIR IN GARLIC FOR ABOUT 1 MINUTE.
STIR IN WINE, SCRAPING ANY BROWNED BITS FROM THE BOTTOM OF THE DISH.
STIR IN BEEF STOCK, THYME AND BAY LEAVES. BRING TO A BOIL; REDUCE HEAT AND SIMMER, STIRRING OCCASIONALLY, UNTIL SLIGHTLY REDUCED, ABOUT 15-20 MINUTES. REMOVE AND DISCARD THYME SPRIGS AND BAY LEAVES.
STIR IN BALSAMIC VINEGAR; SEASON WITH SALT & PEPPER, TO TASTE.
TOP WITH BAGUETTE SLICES TO COVER THE SURFACE OF THE SOUP COMPLETELY; SPRINKLE WITH CHEESES.
PLACE INTO OVEN AND BROIL UNTIL GOLDEN BROWN AND CHEESES HAVE MELTED; ABOUT 3-5 MINUTES.
SERVE IMMEDIATELY.

Lamb Stew With Guinness

RECIPE SUPPLIED BY: GRAHAM
ABOARD : SYLVIA JANE

Ingredients

600G LAMB NECK, TRIM OFF EXCESS FAT & CUT INTO CHUNKS
2 LEEKS, CHOPPED
300G CARROTS, HALVED LENGTHWAYS
300G SWEDE, PEELED AND CUT INTO 2CM PIECES
300ML GUINNESS
400ML LAMB STOCK
FLOUR TO THICKEN
SERVE WITH MASHED POTATO AND PEAS

Method

HEAT THE OVEN TO 190C/FAN 170C/GAS 5.
PUT ALL THE STEW INGREDIENTS IN A LARGE CASSEROLE
SEASON AND STIR WELL.
PUT A SHEET OF FOIL UNDER THE LID TO CREATE A TIGHTER SEAL,
THEN FIRMLY PUSH THE LID DOWN. COOK IN THE OVEN FOR 1 HOUR.
MASH THE FLOUR AND BUTTER TOGETHER UNTIL A SMOOTH PASTE.
AFTER AN HOUR OF COOKING
STIR THE FLOUR MIXTURE INTO THE STEW AND PUT BACK INTO THE
OVEN, UNCOVERED, FOR ANOTHER 30 MINUTES-1 HOUR
OR UNTIL THE LAMB IS TENDER AND THE STEW HAS THICKENED.
STIR IN A FEW FRESH THYME LEAVES
SERVE WITH MASHED POTATO AND PEAS.

One Pot Lime Chicken

RECIPE SUPPLIED BY: PAULA
ABOARD : THE DUKE

Ingredients

1/4 CUP CHOPPED FRESH CORIANDER LEAVES
3 TABLESPOONS EXTRA VIRGIN OLIVE OIL
2 TABLESPOONS FRESHLY SQUEEZED LIME JUICE
1 TABLESPOON LIME ZEST
2 TEASPOONS CHILI POWDER
1 TEASPOON GROUND CUMIN
1 TEASPOON SALT
1 TEASPOON FRESHLY GROUND BLACK PEPPER
2 POUNDS BONELESS, SKINLESS CHICKEN THIGHS

Method

IN A MEDIUM BOWL, COMBINE CORIANDER, 2 TABLESPOONS OLIVE OIL, LIME JUICE, LIME ZEST, CHILI POWDER, CUMIN, SALT AND PEPPER.
IN A LARGE BOWL, COMBINE CHICKEN AND CORIANDER MIXTURE; MARINATE FOR AT LEAST 2 HOURS TO OVERNIGHT, TURNING OCCASIONALLY. DRAIN THE CHICKEN FROM THE MARINADE.

HEAT REMAINING 1 TABLESPOON OLIVE OIL IN A CAST IRON GRILL PAN OVER MEDIUM-HIGH HEAT.* WORKING IN BATCHES, ADD CHICKEN TO THE GRILL PAN IN A SINGLE LAYER AND COOK UNTIL GOLDEN BROWN & COOKED THROUGH, ABOUT 4-5 MINUTES PER SIDE. THEN SERVE

Leek, Mushroom & Pea Pasta

RECIPE SUPPLIED BY: AMANDA
ABOARD : PIXIE

Ingredients

2 X LEEKS WHOLE, THINLY SLICED
2 X GARLIC CLOVES, THINLY SLICED
300 G WHOLEMEAL SPAGHETTI
200 G BUTTON MUSHROOMS SLICED
1 TSP DRIED MIXED HERBS
¼ TSP DRIED CHILLI FLAKES
1½ TBS LEMON JUICE
1 TBS FRESH LEMON RIND GRATED
150 ML UNSWEETENED ALMOND MILK
1 X VEGETABLE STOCK CUBE (TO MAKE 650ML STOCK)
100 G FROZEN GREEN PEAS
1 TBS FRESH FLAT-LEAF PARSLEY
OIL SPRAY

Method

IN A MEDIUM BOWL, COMBINE CORIANDER, 2 TABLESPOONS OLIVE OIL, LIME JUICE, LIME ZEST, CHILI POWDER, CUMIN, SALT AND PEPPER.
IN A LARGE BOWL, COMBINE CHICKEN AND CORIANDER MIXTURE; MARINATE FOR AT LEAST 2 HOURS TO OVERNIGHT, TURNING OCCASIONALLY. DRAIN THE CHICKEN FROM THE MARINADE.

HEAT REMAINING 1 TABLESPOON OLIVE OIL IN A CAST IRON GRILL PAN OVER MEDIUM-HIGH HEAT.* WORKING IN BATCHES, ADD CHICKEN TO THE GRILL PAN IN A SINGLE LAYER AND COOK UNTIL GOLDEN BROWN & COOKED THROUGH, ABOUT 4-5 MINUTES PER SIDE. THEN SERVE

Shakshuka

RECIPE SUPPLIED BY: ALICE
ABOARD : GULLIVER

Ingredients

2 TBSP OLIVE OIL
2 ONIONS, THINLY SLICED
1 RED PEPPER, SLICED
1 YELLOW PEPPER, SLICED
1 RED CHILLI, DESEEDED AND FINELY CHOPPED
4 GARLIC CLOVES, CRUSHED
200G TIN CHOPPED TOMATOES
1 TSP SALT
¼ TSP GROUND BLACK PEPPER
½ TSP GROUND CUMIN
½ TSP GROUND CORIANDER
4 EGGS
FRESH PARSLEY, CHOPPED, TO GARNISH

Method

HEAT THE OIL IN A LARGE, HEAVY-BASED FRYING PAN, ADD THE ONIONS AND COOK GENTLY FOR 5 MINUTES, UNTIL SOFTENED BUT NOT COLOURED.

ADD THE PEPPERS AND CHILLI, THEN COVER AND COOK FOR 8 MINUTES OR UNTIL THE PEPPERS ARE JUST TENDER.

STIR IN THE GARLIC, CHOPPED TOMATOES, SALT AND SPICES, THEN COVER AGAIN AND COOK FOR 8-10 MINUTES, UNTIL THE SAUCE HAS THICKENED.

USING THE BACK OF A TABLESPOON, MAKE 4 INDENTATIONS IN AMONGST THE VEGETABLES AND CAREFULLY BREAK AN EGG INTO EACH ONE.

COVER AND COOK OVER A LOW HEAT FOR ABOUT 5 MINUTES, BASTING OCCASIONALLY WITH THE JUICES, UNTIL THE EGGS HAVE SET. (IF YOU PREFER THE EGGS SCRAMBLED, YOU CAN MIX THEM WITH A FORK BEFORE COVERING THE PAN.)

SPRINKLE WITH CHOPPED PARSLEY AND SERVE.

SERVE WITH SALAD AND WARM PITTA BREAD.

Chicken & Rice Dinner

RECIPE SUPPLIED BY: CHARLIE
ABOARD : JACK O' LANTERN

Ingredients

4 X SKINLESS CHICKEN BREAST CUT LENGTHWISE
1 TABLESPOON VEGETABLE OIL
1 CAN CONDENSED CREAM OF CHICKEN SOUP
1 1/2 CUPS WATER
1/4 TEASPOON PAPRIKA
2 CUPS UNCOOKED INSTANT WHITE RICE
(FOR CREAMIER RICE, DECREASE TO 1 1/2 CUPS)
2 CUPS BROCCOLI FLORETS (ABOUT 6 OUNCES)

Method

SEASON THE CHICKEN WITH SALT AND PEPPER.
HEAT THE OIL IN A 12-INCH PAN OVER MEDIUM-HIGH HEAT.
ADD THE CHICKEN AND COOK FOR 6 MINUTES
UNTIL BROWNED ON BOTH SIDES.
REMOVE THE CHICKEN FROM THE PAN.
STIR THE SOUP, WATER AND PAPRIKA IN THE PAN AND HEAT TO A BOIL.
STIR IN THE RICE AND BROCCOLI. REDUCE THE HEAT TO LOW.
RETURN THE CHICKEN TO THE PAN.
SPRINKLE THE CHICKEN WITH ADDITIONAL PAPRIKA.
COVER AND COOK FOR 5 MINUTES OR UNTIL THE CHICKEN IS DONE AND
THE RICE IS TENDER.
SEASON TO TASTE BEFORE SERVING.

One Pot Sausage & Fish

RECIPE SUPPLIED BY: MARK
ABOARD : BLUE BELLE

Ingredients

15ML EXTRA-VIRGIN OLIVE OIL, PLUS MORE FOR GARNISH
250G ITALIAN HOT SAUSAGE OR CHORIZO
2 LARGE CLOVES GARLIC
1 MEDIUM ONION
750G CHERRY POTATOES, THINLY SLICED
SALT AND FRESHLY GROUND BLACK PEPPER
125ML DRY VERMOUTH OR DRY WHITE WINE
500G CHERRY TOMATOES, HALVED
4 HADDOCK OR COD FILLETS
A HANDFUL FLAT-LEAF PARSLEY, CHOPPED
1/2 LEMON

Method

HEAT 15ML OF EXTRA-VIRGIN OLIVE OIL OVER MEDIUM-HIGH HEAT. ADD THE SAUSAGE TO THE PAN AND CRUMBLE WHILE BROWNING, ABOUT 3 TO 4 MINUTES. WHILE THE SAUSAGE BROWNS, CRUSH THE GARLIC.
THEN ADD THINLY SLICED THE ONION AND THE GARLIC, AND POTATOES TO THE PAN WITH THE SAUSAGE AND SEASON WITH SALT AND PEPPER, TO TASTE. POUR IN HALF OF THE VERMOUTH OR WINE, COVER THE PAN WITH A LID AND COOK 10 TO 12 MINUTES.

ADD THE TOMATOES AND GENTLY STIR INTO THE POTATOES. SET FILLETS ON TOP OF THE POTATOES AND DOUSE WITH THE REMAINING VERMOUTH OR WINE. SEASON THE FISH WITH SALT AND PEPPER, TO TASTE. SET LID IN PLACE AND COOK FOR ABOUT 6 TO 8 MINUTES.

TOP THE FISH WITH PARSLEY, THE JUICE OF 1/2 A LEMON AND GARNISH WITH A LIBERAL DRIZZLE OF EXTRA-VIRGIN OLIVE OIL.

TO SERVE, TRANSFER THE FISH AND SAUSAGE MIXTURE FROM THE PAN INTO SHALLOW BOWLS TO HOLD THE JUICE. SERVE WITH CRUSTY BREAD

29

Mushroom Stroganoff

RECIPE SUPPLIED BY: HEATHER

ABOARD : DAISY

Ingredients

2 TABLESPOONS OLIVE OIL, DIVIDED
1 MEDIUM ONION, DICED
350 G MUSHROOMS, SLICED
3 CLOVES GARLIC
½ TEASPOON DRIED THYME
¼ TEASPOON PEPPER
½ TEASPOON SALT
¼ CUP DRY WHITE WINE(60 ML)
½ TABLESPOON VEGAN WORCESTERSHIRE
¼ CUP FLOUR(30 G)
2 CUPS VEGETABLE BROTH(480 ML)
1 ½ CUPS ALMOND MILK(360 ML)
225 G FUSILLI PASTA, UNCOOKED
FRESH PARSLEY, CHOPPED, FOR SERVING, GARNISH

Method

IN A LARGE POT, HEAT 1 TABLESPOON OF OLIVE OIL OVER MEDIUM HEAT. ONCE THE OIL BEGINS TO SHIMMER, ADD THE ONION AND COOK FOR 3-4 MINUTES, UNTIL SEMI-TRANSLUCENT.
ADD MUSHROOMS AND COOK UNTIL MOST JUICES HAVE EVAPORATED. WITH YOUR SPOON, MAKE A SPACE IN THE CENTER OF THE POT. DRIZZLE IN THE REMAINING TABLESPOON OF OLIVE OIL AND ADD THE GARLIC, THYME, PEPPER, AND SALT.
COOK FOR 2-3 MINUTES, UNTIL FRAGRANT. THEN, ADD THE WHITE WINE AND VEGAN WORCESTERSHIRE SAUCE AND STIR.
ADD FLOUR AND STIR UNTIL FULLY COMBINED. THEN ADD THE VEGETABLE BROTH, ALMOND MILK, AND PASTA, AND STIR
COVER AND INCREASE THE HEAT TO MEDIUM-HIGH.
LET COOK FOR 10-15 MINUTES, OR UNTIL THE LIQUID IS CREAMY AND PASTA IS COOKED.
SERVE IMMEDIATELY, GARNISHED WITH PARSLEY.

One Pot Fish Curry

RECIPE SUPPLIED BY: WENDY
ABOARD : SUNFLOWER

Ingredients

OLIVE OIL
1 LARGE ONION (FINELY CHOPPED)
1 GARLIC CLOVE (MINCED)
1 TSP GROUND TURMERIC
1 TSP GARAM MASALA
400 ML COCONUT MILK
400 G FISH (COD,SALMON & SMOKED HADDOCK)
200 G FROZEN PEAS

Method

HEAT THE OIL IN A LARGE FRYING PAN OVER MEDIUM HEAT. COOK
THE ONION FOR 3 MINUTES UNTIL SOFT.

ADD IN THE GARLIC AND SPICES AND COOK FOR A FURTHER MINUTE.
ADD A SPLASH OF WATER TO PREVENT THEM FROM STICKING.

POUR IN THE COCONUT MILK AND BRING THE MIXTURE TO A BOIL.
COVER AND SIMMER FOR 10 MINUTES.

ADD IN THE FISH MIX AND PEAS AND COOK FOR ABOUT 3 MINUTES
UNTIL THE FISH IS STARTING TO FLAKE.
SERVE STRAIGHT AWAY WITH RICE.

Beef In Cider

RECIPE SUPPLIED BY: SANDY
ABOARD : SMOKEY JOE

Ingredients

900 G STEAK, CUT INTO LARGE CHUNKS
225 G STREAKY BACON IN ONE PIECE
110 G DARK FLAT MUSHROOMS, SLICED
SALT AND FRESHLY MILLED BLACK PEPPER
BEEF DRIPPING
1 MEDIUM ONION, PEELED AND SLICED
350 G SMALL ONIONS, PEELED AND LEFT WHOLE
1 ROUNDED TABLESPOON PLAIN FLOUR
450 ML DRY CIDER
2 CLOVES GARLIC, CHOPPED
2 SPRIGS FRESH THYME (OR ½ TEASPOON DRIED)
1 BAY LEAF

Method

START OFF BY MELTING SOME BEEF DRIPPING IN A VERY LARGE
SOLID FRYING PAN AND FRYING THE SLICED ONION FOR 5 MINUTES.
THEN TURN THE HEAT RIGHT UP, ADD THE CUBES OF MEAT AND
BROWN THEM QUICKLY ON ALL SIDES, TOSSING THEM AROUND
FREQUENTLY. NEXT SPRINKLE IN THE FLOUR, STIR IT AROUND TO
SOAK UP ALL THE JUICES, THEN GRADUALLY POUR IN THE CIDER –
STIRRING ALL THE TIME – AND ADD THE CHOPPED GARLIC AND
HERBS. SEASON WITH SALT AND PEPPER, THEN POUR THE WHOLE LOT
INTO A CASSEROLE, PUT THE LID ON AND COOK IN THE OVEN FOR 2
HOURS.
NOW, USING A BIT MORE BEEF DRIPPING, FRY THE SMALL ONIONS
AND BACON TO COLOUR THEM LIGHTLY, AND ADD THEM TO THE
CASSEROLE TOGETHER WITH THE SLICED MUSHROOMS. THEN PUT
THE LID BACK ON AND COOK FOR A FURTHER HOUR. THIS IS NICE
SERVED WITH NOODLES OR ONION-FLAVOURED RICE.

One Pot Cajun Chicken

RECIPE SUPPLIED BY: FRANCO
ABOARD : DRAGONFLY

Ingredients

500G DICED CHICKEN BREASTS OR THIGHS
2 PEPPERS
1 RED ONION
CAJUN SEASONING
175G RICE
350G WATER
1 SMALL TIN SWEETCORN

Method

DE-SEED AND CUT THE PEPPERS INTO ROUGH CHUNKS.
PEEL AND SLICE THE ONION.
FOR THE CAJUN SEASONING, YOU CAN BUY A PACKET OR POT OR
MIX TOGETHER 2 TSP SALT, 2 TSP GARLIC POWDER, 3 TSP PAPRIKA,
1 TSP PEPPER, 1 TSP ONION POWDER, 1 TSP CAYENNE PEPPER, 1
TSP OREGANO AND 1 TSP THYME, AND ADD RED PEPPER FLAKES
FOR AN EXTRA KICK.
IN A BAKING DISH, ADD CHICKEN, CHOPPED VEG & SWEETCORN.
ADD IN THE RICE.
MIX TOGETHER AND ADD ON THE SEASONING AND MIX AGAIN.
POUR OVER THE WATER.
TIGHTLY COVER WITH FOIL AND BAKE AT 200 DEGREES FOR 35-40
MINUTES

Mexican Beef Stew

RECIPE SUPPLIED BY: STANLEY
ABOARD : KINGFISHER

Ingredients

1 TBSP OIL
350G BEEF CUT INTO STRIPS
1 RED ONION, CUT INTO WEDGES
30G CORIANDER, LEAVES AND STALKS SEPARATED
95G JAR CHIPOTLE CHILLI AND SMOKED PAPRIKA PASTE
400G TIN BUTTER BEANS, DRAINED

Method

HEAT THE OIL IN A LARGE FRYING PAN, WHEN HOT ADD THE BEEF AND ONION WEDGES AND STIR FRY FOR 5 MINS, UNTIL THE BEEF IS BROWN AND THE ONION BEGINNING TO COLOUR.

FINELY CHOP THE CORIANDER STALKS AND ADD TO THE PAN, ALONG WITH THE PAPRIKA AND CHILLI CHIPOTLE SAUCE. FILL THE SAUCE JAR WITH FRESHLY BOILED WATER AND ADD TO THE PAN WITH A FURTHER 2 JARS OF WATER. BRING TO A SIMMER.

STIR THE BUTTER BEANS INTO THE STEW, SEASON WITH PLENTY OF SALT AND PEPPER, WARM THROUGH FOR 2 MINS, OR UNTIL THE BEANS ARE HOT. REMOVE FROM THE HEAT, STIR THROUGH THE CORIANDER AND SERVE.

One Pot Chicken, Sausage & Sprouts

RECIPE SUPPLIED BY: BEN
ABOARD : MISTY

Ingredients

450G BRUSSELS SPROUTS, TRIMMED AND HALVED
5 MEDIUM SHALLOTS, PEELED AND QUARTERED
1 LEMON, THINLY SLICED
3 TABLESPOONS (45ML) EXTRA VIRGIN OLIVE OIL
SALT AND FRESHLY GROUND BLACK PEPPER
3 MEDIUM CLOVES GARLIC, MINCED OR GRATED
1 1/2 TABLESPOONS (20ML) DIJON MUSTARD
1 1/2 TABLESPOONS (20ML) HONEY
1 TABLESPOON (15ML) WORCESTERSHIRE SAUCE
3 TEASPOONS CHOPPED FRESH ROSEMARY NEEDLE
4 CHICKEN THIGHS (ABOUT 680G)
4 LARGE ITALIAN SAUSAGES (ABOUT 680G)
CUT INTO 2-INCH LENGTHS

Method

PLACE RACK IN LOWER THIRD OF OVEN & HEAT TO 230°C
IN A 12-INCH PAN, COMBINE BRUSSELS SPROUTS, SHALLOTS, AND
LEMON WITH 2 TABLESPOONS (30ML) OIL.
SEASON TO TASTE WITH SALT AND PEPPER AND TOSS TO COAT.
IN A SMALL BOWL, COMBINE GARLIC, MUSTARD, HONEY,
WORCESTERSHIRE SAUCE, ROSEMARY, AND REMAINING 1
TABLESPOON (15ML) OIL. SEASON WITH SALT AND PEPPER AND STIR
TO FORM A PASTE. RUB PASTE ALL OVER CHICKEN. NESTLE CHICKEN
AND SAUSAGE PIECES ON TOP OF BRUSSELS SPROUTS.
ROAST ON LOWER RACK UNTIL BRUSSELS SPROUTS ARE BROWNED
AND TENDER FOR ABOUT 25 TO 30 MINUTES. (IF CHICKEN AND
SAUSAGE ARE DONE BEFORE SPROUTS HAVE BROWNED ENOUGH, YOU
CAN TRANSFER THE MEAT TO A PLATE AND LET THE VEGETABLES
FINISH IN THE OVEN; RECOMBINE BEFORE SERVING.) SERVE.

Chicken And Chorizo Rice

RECIPE SUPPLIED BY: CAITLIN
ABOARD : CAROLINE

Ingredients

1 ONION, PEELED AND SLICED
HANDFUL OF CHOPPED CHORIZO
AROUND 400G CHICKEN THIGH FILLETS, CUT INTO BITE SIZE
PIECES CAN SWAP FOR CHICKEN BREAST OR PORK
1 RED PEPPER, DESEEDED AND DICED
1 TIN SWEETCORN, DRAINED
1 TABLESPOON OLIVE OIL
2 CLOVES OF CRUSHED/CHOPPED GARLIC
2 TABLESPOON TOMATO PURÉE
750ML CHICKEN OR VEGETABLE STOCK
300G LONG GRAIN RICE

Method

IN A LARGE FRYING OR SAUCE PAN WITH A LID ADD THE OLIVE OIL
OVER A MEDIUM HEAT.
ADD THE ONIONS AND FRY FOR 5 MINUTES OR UNTIL SOFTENED.
ADD THE GARLIC AND FRY FOR A FURTHER ONE MINUTE.
ADD THE CHICKEN, RED PEPPER AND CHORIZO.
FRY FOR ANOTHER 5 MINUTES AND THEN ADD THE TOMATO PUREE
AND STIR EVERYTHING TOGETHER.
ADD THE RICE AND THE STOCK AND BRING TO THE BOIL.
COVER AND ALLOW TO SIMMER FOR 10 TO 15 MINUTES OR UNTIL THE
RICE HAS ADSORBED MOST OF THE STOCK.
STIR IN THE SWEETCORN AND ALLOW TO REST FOR 5 MINUTES.
SEASON TO TASTE WITH SALT, PEPPER AND OPTIONALLY SOME
PARSLEY OR CORIANDER. YOU COULD ALSO ADD LEMON JUICE.

The Following Recipes Are Quick & Easy Ideal For Those Days When Time Is Short, And You May Not Have A Lot In The Cupboards

Chicken and Potato Traybake

RECIPE SUPPLIED BY: PATRICA
ABOARD : MISTREL

Ingredients

2 TBSP OLIVE OIL
1 TBSP CAJUN OR BARBECUE SEASONING
950G CHICKEN DRUMSTICKS & THIGHS
2 POTATOES 500G
2 BELL PEPPERS , DICED

Method

MIX TOGETHER THE CHICKEN, OIL AND SEASONING.
PLACE IN A LARGE NON-STICK ROASTING TRAY, COVER WITH
FOIL & BAKE IN A PREHEATED OVEN AT 180C FOR ONE HOUR.
POUR OVER BOTH POTATOES AND THE PEPPERS.

MIX TOGETHER THE INGREIDENTS & RETURN TO THE OVEN
COOK UNCOVERED AT 200C FOR HALF AN HOUR,
REMOVE FROM THE OVEN & STIR, BEFORE RETURNING
FOR A FURTHER HALF AN HOUR.

Cheesy Tuna Pasta

RECIPE SUPPLIED BY: ANDY
ABOARD : PANDORA

Ingredients

75G PASTA
1 SMALL TIN OF TUNA, DRAINED
HANDFUL OF SWEETCORN TIN OR FROZEN
HANDFUL OF SPINACH FRESH OR FROZEN
HANDFUL OF GRATED CHEESE
1 TOMATO OR FEW CHERRY TOMATOES
1 TABLESPOON SOFT CHEESE
SALT & PEPPER TO TASTE

Method

COOK THE PASTA IN A SAUCEPAN OF BOILING WATER
THREE MINUTES BEFORE THE END OF COOKING, ADD THE
SWEETCORN AND SPINACH TO THE PASTA. IF USING FROZEN,
ADD 5 MINUTES BEFORE.
DRAIN THE PASTA, SWEETCORN AND SPINACH AND RETURN
TO THE PAN OVER A LOW HEAT.
ADD IN THE GRATED AND SOFT CHEESE AND STIR
THROUGH THE PASTA UNTIL MIXED AND MELTED.

Melanies Jambalaya

Ingredients

CHICKEN - CUBED
CHORIZO SAUSAGE
BELL PEPPER
MUSHROOMS
ONIONS
CHILLIS
1 X PACKET PRE-COOKED MEXICAN RICE
HALF TIN OF SWEETCORN

Method

FRY OFF CUBED CHICKEN BREAST AND CHORIZO,
ADD PEPPERS, CHILLI'S ONIONS AND MUSHROOMS.
COOK UNTIL CHICKEN COOKED.
ADD A PACKET OF PRE-COOKED MEXICAN RICE
ADD HALF TIN SWEETCORN.
COOK ON A LOW HEAT UNTIL WARMED THROUGH.
ENJOY!

Balsamic Chicken and Veggies

RECIPE SUPPLIED BY: PATRICK
ABOARD : TAVISTOCK BELLE

Ingredients

CHICKEN BREAST FILLETS
ITALIAN SALAD DRESSING
BALSAMIC VINEGAR
HONEY
CHILLI FLAKES OR PAPRIKA
ASPARAGUS
CARROTS
TOMATOES

Method

WHISK TOGETHER SALAD DRESSING, BALSAMIC VINEGAR,
HONEY AND CHILLI FLAKSE OR PAPRIKA.
SEASON CHICKEN WITH SALT AND PEPPER AND FRY 7 MINUTES
ADD HALF THE DRESSING MIXTURE TO THE PAN AND TOSS
REMOVE CHICKEN FROM PAN AND SET ASIDE.
ADD CARROTS AND ASPARAGUS TO THE PAN AND COOK UNTIL
CRISP TENDER.
TRANSFER VEGGIES TO THE PLATE OF CHICKEN,
THEN ADD REMAINING DRESSING TO PAN, COOK UNTIL
THICKENED.ADD TOMATOES TO PLATE WITH
CHICKEN AND VEGGIES, THEN TOSS EVERYTHING
WITH THE DRESSING IN THE PAN.

Sweet & Sour Pork

RECIPE SUPPLIED BY: PAULINE
ABOARD : THE WOODSMAN

Ingredients

BELLY PORK - CUBED
ONION - CHOPPED
SMALL TIN OF PINEAPPLE (IN JUICE, OR
BETTER STILL, FRESH PINEAPPLE
1 BELL PEPPER
TOMATO KETCHUP
BRANSTON PICKLE
SUGAR, SALT & PEPPER

Method

BROWN THE BELLY PORK UTIL SEALED. PUT ON A PLATE.
SWEAT A CHOPPED ONION IN A LITTLE OIL.
ADD THE TIN OF PINEAPPLE AND THE CHOPPED PEPPER,
ADD A GOOD SQUEEZE OF TOMATO KETCHUP
A TABLESPOON OF PICKLE (BRANSTON PREFERABLY),
A TABLESPOON OF SUGAR AND SOME SALT AND PEPPER
MIX A DESSERTSPOON OF CORNFLOUR WITH TWO OF MALT VINEGAR
ADD TO THE PAN WITH PINEAPPLE JUICE AND THE BROWNED PORK,
ADD SOME WATER TO IT SO IT'S A NICE THICK SAUCE.
LET IT SIMMER FOR AN HOUR OR SO UNTIL PORK IS TENDER.
CHECK THE TASTE, ADD MORE VINEGAR/SUGAR TO GET THE
SWEET / SOUR BALANCE JUST RIGHT.
SERVE WITH RICE OR A BREAD OF YOUR CHOICE.

Chicken And Pepperoni BBQ Melt

RECIPE SUPPLIED BY: TONY
ABOARD : WOODSTOCK

Ingredients

500 G CHICKEN FILLETS
PEPPERONI SLICES
1 RED PEPPER
GRATED CHEESE
BBQ SAUCE
1 ONION

Method

PEEL AND CHOP HALF AN ONION
DE-SEED AND DICE A RED PEPPER.
SLICE PEPPERONI
GRATE CHEESE (IF NOT ALREADY)
TO A BAKING DISH, ADD THE CHICKEN FILLETS
ADD ON THE ONIONS AND PEPPERS
ADD ON THE PEPPERONI
FINISH WITH THE GRATED CHEESE
BAKE AT 170 DEGREES FOR 20 MINUTES.
REMOVE AND ADD BBQ SAUCE AND MIX, RETURN TO OVEN
FOR 5-10 MINUTES UNTIL CHICKEN IS FULLY COOKED
SERVE WITH RICE, PASTA OR MASH.

Sausage & Bean Casserole

RECIPE SUPPLIED BY: JOHN
ABOARD : STELLA

Ingredients

6 PORK SAUSAGES
FOR FRYING OIL
4 RASHERS STREAKY BACON, CHOPPED
1 SMALL ONION, DICED
1 SMALL CARROT, DICED
400G TIN HARICOT BEANS, DRAINED
1 TBSP ENGLISH MUSTARD
1 TBSP SOFT LIGHT BROWN SUGAR
1 TBSP TOMATO PURÉE
200ML CHICKEN STOCK
A HANDFUL FLAT-LEAF PARSLEY, CHOPPED

Method

HEAT THE OVEN TO 200C/FAN 180C/GAS 6.
FRY THE SAUSAGES IN A LITTLE OIL IN A CASSEROLE DISH
REMOVE THE SAUSAGES, THEN ADD THE BACON, ONION & CARROT
COOK FOR 7 MINUTES OR UNTIL EVERYTHING IS BROWNED & THE
BACON IS CRISPING UP.
ADD THE REMAINING INGREDIENTS, EXCEPT THE PARSLEY
SEASON & STIR WELL. RETURN THE SAUSAGES TO THE DISH
THEN COVER AND BAKE FOR 30 MINUTES.
STIR IN THE PARSLEY, TO SERVE.

Stove Top Slow Cooked Beef

RECIPE SUPPLIED BY: EMMA
ABOARD : ROOTS

Ingredients

BEEF - CUBED
ONION - CHOPPED
DICED CARROTS
CELERY
SLAT & PEPPER
BEEF STOCK
DICED POTOTOES
ROOT VEGITABLES OF YOUR CHOICE

Method

FIRST FRY THE ONION AND DICED CARROTS, CELERY
ADD SALT & PEPPER TO TASTE
BROWN THE BEEF AND ADD STOCK TO COVER
LEAVE ON THE STOVE TOP ALL DAY, WITH A LID ON
ADD DICED POTATOES AND ROOT VEG,
SIMMER UNTIL TENDER
SERVE WITH CRUSTY BREAD.
ADD DUMPLINGS 20 MINS BEFORE ,IF YOU LIKE THEM

Pork in Cider

RECIPE SUPPLIED BY: KAREN
ABOARD : CHUFFIN SPARROW

Ingredients

350-400 GM PORK SHOULDER CUT CUBED
1 X TIN CIDER
1 X CLOVE GARLIC
1 X LARGE ONION DICED
2X CARROTS DICED
2 X LARGE POTATOES CUT IN LARGE CHUNKS
SALT X PEPPER TO TASTE
1 X CHICKEN OR HAM STOCK CUBE
3 X TEASPOON CORNFLOWER TO THICKEN

Method

I COOK IT IN A THERMAL POT FOR ABOUT 3 HOURS OR COULD BE
COOKED IN A SLOW COOKER FOR 4 HOURS, A PRESSURE COOKER
FOR 30 MINUTES OR SLOW COOKED ON YOUR LOG BURNER.
FRY THE PORK, ONIONS AND GARLIC FOR A FEW MINUTES
ADD THE REST OF THE INGREDIENTS AND BOIL FOR 10 MINS.
PLACE IN THERMAL POT, OR CASSEROLE DISH FOR 2-3 HOURS

Stove Top Beef Casserole

RECIPE SUPPLIED BY: SUE
ABOARD : EVENING STAR

Ingredients

1 KG DICED BRAISING BEEF
1 LARGE ONION DICED
3 CARROTS CHOPPED
4 STICKS CELERY CHOPPED
A LARGE HANDFUL OF BUTTON MUSHROOMS
1 CLOVE GARLIC CHOPPED
TOMATO PUREE
TIN CHOPPED TOMATOES
WORCESTERSHIRE SAUCE
OIL TO FRY

Method

IN A LARGE POT FRY THE ONIONS, GARLIC.
ADD MEAT LIGHTLY BROWN.
ADD ALL OTHER VEG. ADD ALL OTHER INGREDIENTS. STIR.
COVER WITH WATER SO ALL INGREDIENTS ARE SUBMERGED.
POP ON STOVE TOP WITH A LID FOR ABOUT 3 HOURS.
ADD SEASONING.
OTHER THINGS THAT CAN BE ADDED ARE SWEDE,
DUMPLINGS, NEW POTATOES ETC.

Vegetarian Toad In The Hole

RECIPE SUPPLIED BY:PAULETTE
ABOARD: DOBSONS CHOICE

Ingredients

- 180G PLAIN FLOUR
- 3 LARGE EGGS
- 280ML WHOLE MILK
- 2 TBSP WHOLEGRAIN MUSTARD
- FOR THE FILLING
- 300G BABY CARROTS
- 2 RED ONIONS, PEELED, CUT INTO WEDGES
- 1 RED CHILLI, FINELY SLICED
- 1 TSP PAPRIKA
- 4 TBSP OLIVE OIL
- PACKET OR HOMEMADE ONION GRAVY TO SERVE

Method

HEAT THE OVEN TO 200°C/GAS 6. SIFT THE FLOUR INTO A LARGE
BOWL WITH A PINCH OF SALT. MAKE A WELL IN THE CENTRE, CRACK
IN THE EGGS AND WHISK TO COMBINE.
ADD THE MILK & MIX TO MAKE A BATTER. STIR IN THE MUSTARD,
SEASON WELL, THEN SET THE BATTER ASIDE TO REST.
TOSS THE CARROTS AND ONIONS, CHILLI, PAPRIKA & OIL
IN THE TIN. ROAST FOR 15 MINUTES,INCREASE THE
HEAT TO 220°C/GAS 7 AND POUR THE BATTER OVER.
BAKE FOR 20 MINUTES UNTIL RISEN & GOLDEN
CUT INTO WEDGES AND SERVE WITH GRAVY.

Fruity One Pot Lamb Tagine

RECIPE SUPPLIED BY:ANTHONY
ABOARD: BRIGADOON

Ingredients

600G DICED LAMB STEAKS
3-4 TBLS RAS EL HANOUT SPICE MIX
1 LARGE ONION, DICED
2-3 GARLIC CLOVES, FINELY SLICED
1 TABLESPOON RUNNY HONEY
1 LAMB STOCKCUBE IN 450ML BOILING WATER
100G DRIED APRICOTS, HALVED
400G CAN CHOPPED TOMATOES
COUSCOUS TO SERVE, OPTIONAL
HANDFUL OF FRESH CORIANDER AND MINT LEAVES,
ROUGHLY CHOPPED, OPTIONAL

Method

TOSS THE LAMB IN HALF THE SPICE MIX AND MARINADE FOR AT
LEAST 30 MINS IF POSSIBLE. HEAT 1 TBSP OIL IN A LARGE PAN
ADD THE LAMB AND FRY UNTIL BROWNED ON ALL SIDES.
REMOVE AND SET ASIDE.
ADD THE ONION TO THE PAN WITH THE GARLIC & REMAINING
SPICE MIX & FRY FOR 2-3 MINS UNTIL SOFT.
ADD HONEY, STOCK, TOMATOES AND APRICOTS
RETURN MEAT TO THE PAN.
COVER & COOK GENTLY FOR 1 HOUR OR UNTIL MEAT
IS COOKED AND TENDER.
SERVE GARNISHED WITH THE HERBS &WITH
A BOWL OF COUSCOUS.

One Pot Chicken And Chorizo

RECIPE SUPPLIED BY: PAULA & JAMES
ABOARD: LAZY DAYS

Ingredients

1 TSP OLIVE OIL
150G PACK DICED CHORIZO
3 SKINLESS CHICKEN THIGH FILLETS, SLICED INTO THICK STRIPS
2 ROASTED PEPPERS, SLICED
2 GARLIC CLOVES, CRUSHED
1 X 400G TIN CHOPPED TOMATOES
50G BLACK PITTED OLIVES, HALVED
1 X 215G TIN BUTTER BEANS, RINSED/DRAINED
1 X 100G BAG BABY LEAF SPINACH
SMALL HANDFUL OF CHOPPED PARSLEY

Method

HEAT THE OIL IN A LARGE SAUTÉ PAN & FRY THE CHORIZO FOR 2-3 MINUTES OVER A MEDIUM HEAT UNTIL GOLDEN AND CRISP. REMOVE WITH A SLOTTED SPOON AND SET ASIDE.
SEASON THE CHICKEN, BROWN IN THE FAT REMAINING IN THE PAN ABOUT 6-8 MINUTES ON A HIGH HEAT.
STIR IN THE PEPPERS & GARLIC, FOLLOWED BY THE TOMATOES, OLIVES AND BUTTER BEANS WITH 100ML WATER AND SOME SEASONING. RETURN THE CHORIZO TO THE PAN & SIMMER FOR 8-10 MINUTES UNTIL THICKENED AND RICH.
STIR IN THE SPINACH, LEAVE TO WILT FOR 2 MINS.
SPRINKLE WITH PARSLEY & SERVE.

Asian Style Breakfast Eggs

RECIPE SUPPLIED BY:FRANCIS
ABOARD: SWAN SONG

Ingredients

RED CHILLI
1 TBSP. SUNFLOWER OIL
FRESH GINGER, GRATED
2 EGGS
1 SPRING ONION, FINELY CHOPPED
SESAME SEEDS – BLACK & WHITE, TOASTED

Method

FINELY CHOP THE CHILLI & FRY IN A LITTLE OIL WITH THE GINGER.
CRACK THE TWO EGGS INTO THE PAN
AS SOON AS THEY START TO COOK, TOP WITH SPRING ONIONS
LASTLY THE SESAME SEEDS SO THEY SET INTO THE WHITE.
SERVE IMMEDIATELY.

One Pot Potato Curry

RECIPE SUPPLIED BY:CHLOE
ABOARD: UNCHAINED MELODY

Ingredients

3 TBSP. SUNFLOWER OIL
2 LARGE ONIONS, FINELY CHOPPED
1 CINNAMON STICK
THE SEEDS FROM 8 CARDAMOM PODS
1 BAY LEAF
2 GREEN CHILLIES,DESEEDED AND CHOPPED
1 PACK OF PLUM TOMATOES, CHOPPED
500 G POTATOES, CUT INTO CUBES
1 CAN COCONUT MILK
SALT AND PEPPER
50 ML MILK
2 TBSP. CHOPPED CORIANDER

Method

HEAT THE OIL IN A MEDIUM-SIZED SAUCEPAN AND COOK THE
ONIONS OVER A MEDIUM HEAT, UNTIL THEY ARE SOFT.
ADD THE CINNAMON STICK, CARDAMOM, BAY LEAF, GINGER &
CHILLI, & COOK FOR ANOTHER THREE MINUTES OR SO,
THEN ADD TOMATOES & COOK FOR ANOTHER FOUR MINUTES,
OCCASIONALLY STIRRING.
BOIL THE POTATOES IN THE COCONUT MILK AND
SEASONING FOR 20 MINUTES, ADDING A BIT OF
FULL-FAT MILK IF IT LOOKS A LITTLE DRY.
WHEN POTATOES ARE SOFT ADD THE REST OF
ONIONS, STIR & HEAT THROUGH.
SCATTER WITH THE CORIANDER AND SERVE

One Pot Pork Paella

RECIPE SUPPLIED BY:ANTONIA
ABOARD: JUST CHUGGIN'

Ingredients

1 TBSP OLIVE OIL
500G PORK MINCE
1 ONION, FINELY CHOPPED
35G SACHET PAELLA SEASONING
300G PAELLA RICE OR SHORT GRAIN RICE
300G FROZEN PEAS, BLANCHED

Method

WARM THE OIL IN A LARGE FRYING PAN OR PAELLA PAN.
ADD THE PORK AND CHOPPED ONION AND FRY FOR 5 MINS,
STIRRING FREQUENTLY TO DRIVE TO BROWN THE MEAT.
ADD THE RICE FRY FOR 2 MINS UNTIL YOU CAN HEAR THE RICE
CRACKLING SLIGHTLY. POUR IN 700ML HOT WATER ALONG WITH THE
PAELLA MIX. STIR AND COVER WITH A LID,
ADD MORE WATER IF NECCESARY ,REDUCE THE HEAT TO LOW AND
COOK FOR 15 MINS, OR UNTIL THE RICE IS TENDER.
PUT THE PEAS ON TOP OF THE COOKED PAELLA, GENTLY FORK
THEM THROUGH TO HEAT UP THEM UP. REMOVE THE PAELLA
FROM THE HEAT, AND ALLOW TO REST FOR 5 MINS,
SEASON WITH PLENTY OF SALT AND PEPPER, SERVE

Recipe

Ingredients

Method

Recipe

Ingredients

Method

Recipe

Ingredients

Method

Recipe

Ingredients

Method

Recipe

Ingredients

_____
_____
_____
_____
_____
_____
_____
_____
_____

Method

_____
_____
_____
_____
_____
_____
_____
_____
_____
_____
_____
_____
_____

Recipe

Ingredients

Method

Recipe

Ingredients

_____
_____
_____
_____
_____
_____
_____
_____

Method

_____
_____
_____
_____
_____
_____
_____
_____
_____
_____
_____
_____
_____

Recipe

Ingredients

Method

Recipe

Ingredients

Method

Recipe

Ingredients

Method

Recipe

Ingredients

Method

Recipe

Ingredients

Method

Recipe

Ingredients

Method

Recipe

Ingredients

Method

Recipe

Ingredients

Method

Recipe

Ingredients

Method

Recipe

Ingredients

Method

Recipe

Ingredients

Method

Recipe

Ingredients

Method

Recipe

Ingredients

Method

Recipe

Ingredients

Method

Recipe

Ingredients

Method

Recipe

Ingredients

_____
_____
_____
_____
_____
_____
_____
_____
_____

Method

_____
_____
_____
_____
_____
_____
_____
_____
_____
_____
_____
_____

Recipe

Ingredients

Method

Recipe

Ingredients

Method

INDEX

Printed in Great Britain
by Amazon

13355046R00045